FIFA WOMEN'S WORLD CUP AU·NZ·23™

Kids' HANDBOOK

© FIFA TM

WELBECK

Published in 2023 by Welbeck Children's Books
An Imprint of Welbeck Children's Limited,
part of the Welbeck Publishing Group
Offices in: London - 20 Mortimer Street, London W1T 3JW &
Sydney - Level 17, 207 Kent St, Sydney NSW 2000 Australia
www.welbeckpublishing.com

Design and layout © Welbeck Children's Limited 2023
Text copyright © Welbeck Children's Limited 2023

ISBN 978 1 80453 517 2

10 9 8 7 6 5 4 3 2 1

Printed in Lithuania

Writer: Emily Stead
Senior Commissioning Editor: Suhel Ahmed
Design Manager: Matt Drew
Designer: Ben Ruocco
Picture Researcher: Paul Langan
Consultant: Anthony Hobbs

The publishers would like to thank the following sources for their
kind permission to reproduce the pictures in this book.

The publisher has taken every reasonable step to ensure the
accuracy of the facts contained herein at the time of going
to press, but can take no responsibility for any incorrect
information arising from changes that may take place after this
point. For the latest information, please visit: www.fifa.com/
fifaplus/en/tournaments/womens/womensworldcup/australia-
new-zealand2023.com

The statistics and records in the book are correct as of Feb 2023.

A catalogue record for this book is available from the British Library.

FSC
www.fsc.org
MIX
Paper from
responsible sources
FSC® C107574

The publishers would like to thank the following sources for their
kind permission to reproduce the pictures in this book. (T-top,
B-bottom, L-left, R-right)

GETTY IMAGES: AFP 6T; Gabriel Aponte 24L; Franco Arland/Icon
Sport 32R; Naomi Baker/FIFA 6B, 13, 17B, 19R, 20R, 47; Naomi Baker/
The FA 21L, 31L, 31R; Jose Breton/NurPhoto 35L, 37L, 37R; Simon
Bruty /Sports Illustrated 15B; Lynne Cameron/The FA 18L; Alex
Caparros/FIFA 12; Tony Feder 27; Kieran Galvin/DeFodi Images 23R;
Paul Gilham 16; Patrick Goosen/BSR Agency 35R; David Gray 10;
Laurence Griffiths 18R; Mike Hewitt/FIFA 17T; Ian Hitchcock 8-9;
Chris Hyde 28R; Catherine Ivill/FIFA 38R; Mark Kolbe 28L; Matthew
Lewis/FIFA 29L; Kevin Light 30R; Francisco Macia/Quality Sport
Images 36L; Maryam Majd/ATPImages 5; Marianna Massey/FIFA 46;
Maddie Meyer/FIFA 14-15, 22R, 39R; Jonathan Moscrop 38L; Albert
Perez 4, 25L; Joe Prior/Visionhaus 32L; Quality Sport Images 15T;
Manuel Queimadelos/Quality Sport Images 29R; Vaughn Ridley
20L; Richard Rodriguez 22L; Fran Santiago 34L; Richard Sellers/
Soccrates 7; Brad Smith/ISI Photos 25R, 36R, 39L; Thananuwat
Srirasant 34R; Sarah Stier/UEFA 33L; Boris Streubel 19L, 23L; Luis
Veniegra/SOPA Images 30L; Visionhaus 33R; James Williamson/
AMA 21R, 24R; Zhizhao Wu 45

SHUTTERSTOCK: Taras Vyshnya 9T

CONTENTS

WELCOMING THE WORLD

Throughout July and August, the world's top players will compete for the greatest prize in women's football, at the ninth FIFA Women's World Cup! Packed with profiles of the teams and players, facts, stats, puzzles and activities, this handbook is your complete guide to the tournament. Plus, you can fill in the results charts to record every memorable match! Let's kick off . . .

WHERE IS IT?

Two different nations (Australia and Aotearoa New Zealand) will host the competition, across nine cities and ten stadiums. The city of Sydney on Australia's east coast is the destination for the final.

Co-hosts Australia and Aotearoa New Zealand hope that their home advantage will help them hit top form.

WORLD CUP TRIVIA
Aotearoa is the Māori-language name for New Zealand.

WHEN IS IT?

The action gets underway in Auckland, Aotearoa New Zealand, on 20 July, to begin a month-long feast of football! Mark 20 August on your calendar – that's when the trophy will be won, at Stadium Australia.

WHO'S PLAYING?

The competition has grown from 24 to 32 teams for the first time. There were just 30 places up for grabs for the 172 nations that tried to qualify, alongside the two spots reserved for the host countries. Among the first teams to book their flights were China PR, Korea Republic and Sweden.

China PR earned their place by winning the 2022 AFC Women's Asian Cup.

SPLASH LANDING

Tazuni is a football-loving penguin from the Tasman Sea and the official mascot for the tournament! She is a 15-year-old midfielder, who fell in love with football after playing the game on the beach one day. She is set to welcome teams from around the world and show off her skills, too.

AU·NZ 2023

© FIFA TM

FIFA WOMEN'S CUP 2023 FAN FACTS

Wherever in the world you're watching from, all fans need the fast facts about this year's tournament at their fingertips! Share these gems with your fellow supporters and family.

32 TEAMS will compete for glory in Australia and Aotearoa New Zealand – that's eight more nations than featured at France 2019.

64 MATCHES will be played in total, with New Zealand kicking off the group stage in Auckland, and Sydney hosting what's set to be a fantastic final.

Fans will be treated to at least **5,760 MINUTES** of football – that's before stoppage time and any extra time is played! You'll be in World Cup heaven!

As the women's game continues to grow, the tournament is a global celebration, with teams from **ARGENTINA TO ZAMBIA** competing!

Zambia are playing at the FIFA Women's World Cup for the first time.

Matches are to be played in the **EVENING** (with some exceptions) Down Under, when it will be morning in Europe. American fans will have to set their alarm clocks for an even earlier start!

USA are the defending champions and will not give up their title easily, having won the trophy a record four times.

SEVEN NATIONS

Only seven teams have featured in all nine FIFA Women's World Cup tournaments. Use the flags to help you find the names of the nations in the grid.

_ _ _ _ _ _

_ _ _ _ _ _ _

_ _ _ _ _

_ _ _ _ _ _

_ _ _ _ _ _ _

_ _ _ _ _ _

_ _ _ _ _ _ _   _ _ _ _ _ _

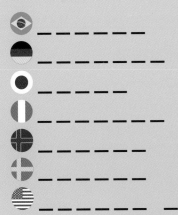

Y	E	G	E	R	M	A	N	Y	S	U	I
H	U	Z	J	X	P	C	R	M	V	N	P
W	P	F	R	M	N	I	G	E	R	I	A
G	C	I	S	B	T	D	I	O	K	T	I
N	O	R	W	A	Y	U	Q	A	P	E	B
M	Z	U	E	Z	R	V	J	Z	K	D	G
B	T	H	D	I	Q	X	V	A	W	S	V
P	R	U	E	W	M	I	G	L	P	T	A
E	M	A	N	X	P	H	E	J	K	A	Z
J	S	F	Z	O	R	A	U	V	Q	T	N
D	X	P	V	I	T	L	N	W	R	E	K
Q	M	H	B	G	L	Z	H	I	C	S	N

STARS, STRIPES AND LIONESSES

Take a look at this scene from when England last faced rivals United States at Wembley. Can you spot six differences in the second picture?

The answers are at the back of the book.

✓

DISCOVER AUSTRALIA AND AOTEAROA NEW ZEALAND

Not one but two nations will host the FIFA Women's World Cup 2023, for a celebration of women's football like never before! Neighbours Australia and Aotearoa New Zealand will jointly stage the competition, as the famous trophy travels to Oceania for the first time. Here's a quick guide to your hosts!

PAST TOURNAMENTS

Australia have appeared at eight FIFA Women's World Cups, while New Zealand have featured six times. Australia's *Matildas* have won seven World Cup games in total. New Zealand's *Football Ferns*, on the other hand, are still looking for their first victory.

CHOSEN CAPTAINS

Striker and all-time top goalscorer Sam Kerr has captained Australia since February 2019, while defender and skipper Ail Riley is set to represent Aotearoa New Zealand at an incredible fifth World Cup. Both Kerr and Riley are among the ten most-capped players for their countries.

SPECIAL CITY

The harbour city of Sydney on Australia's east coast, with its beautiful beaches and iconic landmarks such as the Sydney Harbour Bridge and Opera House, was chosen to host the final. Sydney's Stadium Australia will also stage earlier knockout round fixtures, while Adelaide, Brisbane, Melbourne and Perth are all confirmed as host cities.

NORTH V. SOUTH

The two main islands of Aotearoa New Zealand are called North Island and South Island, while about 700 smaller islands belong to the country. Auckland, Hamilton and Wellington are host cities in the North Island, while the fourth, Dunedin, is in the South Island.

WORLD CUP TRIVIA
New Zealand's best World Cup performance was at Canada 2015, where they drew two of their three matches.

Australia twice beat New Zealand in friendly matches in 2022.

AU·NZ 2023

© FIFA TM

THE STADIUMS

Ten stadiums in nine cities across Australia and Aotearoa New Zealand will host the FIFA Women's World Cup 2023. New Zealand kick off the tournament at Eden Park in Auckland. The final will be staged at the huge Stadium Australia in Sydney.

The Indigenous names of the cities are shown in brackets.

❶ PERTH
(BOORLOO)
STADIUM: Perth Rectangular Stadium
CAPACITY: 22,225
MATCHES: Group stage
FACT: A stadium has stood on the same site for over a century!

❷ ADELAIDE
(TARNTANYA)
STADIUM: Hindmarsh Stadium
CAPACITY: 18,435
MATCHES: Group stage, round of 16
FACT: Thousands of extra seats were added especially for the tournament.

❸ SYDNEY
(GADIGAL)
STADIUM: Stadium Australia & Sydney Football Stadium
CAPACITY: 83,500 & 42,512
MATCHES: Group stage, round of 16, quarter-final, semi-final, final
FACT: The city of Sydney will host Australia's opener against newcomers Republic of Ireland.

Stadium Australia's design include state-of-the-art features that are environmentally friendly.

ANZ Stadium

❹ MELBOURNE
(NAARM)
STADIUM: Melbourne Rectangular Stadium
CAPACITY: 30,052
MATCHES: Group stage, round of 16
FACT: This stadium has won awards for its futuristic design.

❺ BRISBANE
(MEAANJIN)
STADIUM: Brisbane Stadium
CAPACITY: 52,263
MATCHES: Group stage, round of 16, quarter-final, third-place play-off
FACT: Bronze medals will be awarded in Brisbane.

❻ AUCKLAND
(TĀMAKI MAKAURAU)
STADIUM: Eden Park
CAPACITY: 48,276
MATCHES: Group stage, round of 16, quarter-final, semi-final
FACT: New Zealand open the tournament at the historic Eden Park on 20 July.

❼ WELLINGTON
(TE WHANGANUI-A-TARA)
STADIUM: Wellington Regional Stadium
CAPACITY: 39,000
MATCHES: Group stage, round of 16, quarter-final
FACT: New Zealand fans can catch the *Football Ferns'* second group match here.

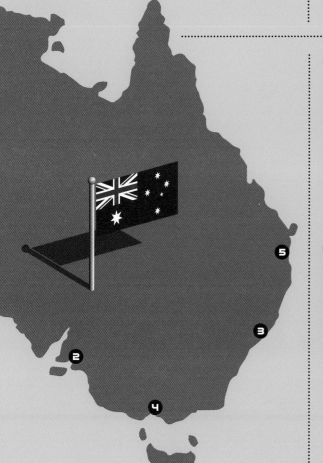

❽ HAMILTON
(KIRIKIRIROA)
STADIUM: Waikato Stadium
CAPACITY: 25,111
MATCHES: Group stage
FACT: Rugby matches are also held here.

❾ DUNEDIN
(ŌTEPOTI)
STADIUM: Dunedin Stadium
CAPACITY: 28,744
MATCHES: Group stage
FACT: Ten different nations from Groups A, C, E and G will visit Dunedin.

DESTINATION: SYDNEY

With qualification completed, teams could begin to dream of World Cup glory! To reach the final in Sydney, sides must play six matches – three group matches followed by three knockout ties. Then it's all to play for in the famous final!

GROUP STAGE

The 32 teams are organised into eight groups of four. The two host countries are kept apart, and grouped with sides from around the world. Each team has to play the others in its group once, with the top two teams from each group going through to the round of 16.

England's Lucy Bronze loves scoring important goals on the world stage.

ROUND OF 16

The eight group winners and eight runners-up head to the first knockout round, the round of 16. From this round on, matches cannot end in a draw, and can go to extra time and even penalties to decide the winning team.

QUARTER-FINALS

The final eight teams face off in four quarter-finals, in the cities of Wellington and Auckland in Aotearoa New Zealand, and Brisbane and Sydney in Australia. The only African nation to ever reach the quarter-finals so far was Nigeria, at the FIFA Women's World Cup in 1999.

WORLD CUP TRIVIA
The 2019 clash between finalists USA and the Netherlands drew a record global audience of 1.12 billion viewers.

SEMI-FINALS

United States have an unstoppable semi-finals record, having made the final four teams in all eight tournaments to date. With so much at stake, semi-finals are often nerve-racking affairs with close scorelines. The Australian cities of Sydney and Auckland will host the two contests.

THE FINAL

The spectacular FIFA Women's World Cup final is the biggest match in women's international football and a real celebration of the game. Millions of fans tune in from all over the globe. Extra time has been needed in three of the eight finals played so far, with Japan and United States requiring penalty shoot-outs to take gold.

FINAL SCORES

Year	Teams	Score
1991	United States	2
	Norway	1
1995	Norway	2
	Germany	0
1999	United States	0
	China PR	0
	(5–4 pens)	
2003	Germany	2
	Sweden	1
	(AET)	
2007	Germany	2
	Brazil	0
2011	Japan	2
	United States	2
	(3–1 pens)	
2015	United States	5
	Japan	2
2019	United States	2
	Netherlands	0

AU·NZ 2023

© FIFA TM

Captain Megan Rapinoe's (15) spot-kick helped USA defeat the Netherlands 2-0 in the 2019 final.

TOP TROPHIES

As well as the top prize, the famous FIFA Women's World Cup Trophy, more accolades are awarded to the tournament's special players and performances. Here's a look at what's on offer in 2023 and who won what last time around.

ADIDAS GOLDEN GLOVE

This award is presented to the best no.1 in the world! The number of clean sheets as well as technical skills are scored by the judges, while keepers can also be considered for the Golden Ball award. Netherlands skipper Sari van Veenendaal was the winner in 2019.

Sari van Veenendaal (L), Megan Rapinoe (C) and Alex Morgan (R) with their trophies following the final of the FIFA Women's World Cup 2019™.

ADIDAS GOLDEN BOOT

USA's Megan Rapinoe pipped team-mate Alex Morgan and England's Ellen White to the award for the tournament's top goalscorer in 2019. All three players scored six goals, the two Americans added three assists each, but Rapinoe won the trophy by taking fewer minutes to reach her tally. Morgan was awarded the Silver Boot, while White claimed the Bronze Boot.

FIFA YOUNG PLAYER AWARD

Giulia Gwinn (R) was awarded the Young Player Award at France 2019, a prize given to the tournament's best young player aged 21 or under. The prize's only previous winners were teenagers Kadeisha Buchanan (2015) and Caitlin Foord (2011), who are now both superstars for their nations.

FIFA FAIR PLAY AWARD

France won this award, which recognises fair play, at the previous two World Cups. Teams must have the best fair play record in the tournament, which may mean they received the fewest yellow and red cards or committed the fewest fouls. To have a chance of winning, teams must reach the knockout rounds.

QUICK QUIZ

Answer true or false to these questions all about the prizes awarded at France 2019.

		TRUE	FALSE
❶	The Golden Boot winner scored six goals and provided three assists.	☐	☐
❷	United States won the Fair Play Award at France 2019.	☐	☐
❸	No nation has won the Young Player Award more than once.	☐	☐
❹	Germany's goalkeeper won the Golden Glove at France 2019.	☐	☐

Answers at the back of the book.

FIFA Women's World Cup France 2019™ adidas

ADIDAS GOLDEN BALL

Megan Rapinoe had the golden touch at France 2019, winning the Golden Ball for the Outstanding Player of the Tournament, the Golden Boot and the World Cup trophy itself! Silver and Bronze Ball trophies are also awarded to the second- and third-best players.

HISTORY-MAKERS

Here are just some of the incredible records set by terrific teams and superstar players at the FIFA Women's World Cup. How many of these trailblazing stats do you know?

4
Only four nations have been World Cup winners in the competition's history: Norway, Germany, Japan and United States.

13-0
United States set a tournament record victory at France 2019. It was also the most goals scored by a team in a World Cup match.

146
Canada 2015 and France 2019 share the record for the highest-scoring goals in a single tournament. Goals galore!

90,185
The 1999 World Cup final between United States and China PR saw a bumper crowd pack into the Rose Bowl, Pasadena, USA.

622
German goalkeeper Nadine Angerer (R) once went 622 minutes without letting in a goal. The length of time equates to more than six matches. Champions Germany didn't concede a single goal in the 2007 tournament! Wow!

17
Brazilian Marta is the tournament's all-time top scorer, with a jaw-dropping 17 goals.

5 It took Swiss scorer Fabienne Humm (R) a matter of minutes to bag the World Cup's fastest hat-trick against Ecuador at Canada 2015.

10 USA forward Michelle Akers is the only player to reach double figures for goals in a single tournament back at China 1991. Legend!

16 At 16 years and 34 days Nigeria's teenage star Ifeanyi Chiejine became the World Cup's youngest-ever player at USA 1999.

7 Brazil's Formiga (L) famously played in a record number of tournaments over a period of 24 years! She's also the oldest player at a World Cup, and was 41 years, 112 days when she played her last match at France 2019.

GOALKEEPERS

As the last line of defence, goalkeepers must stay alert for 90 minutes and beyond to make key saves at any moment. Shot-stopping, penalty-saving, catching and kicking are all skills that a no.1 needs to keep her team out of danger. Here are four stoppers set to shine at the 2023 tournament.

SANDRA **PAÑOS**

Paños started out as a futsal goalkeeper, a skilful game played with a smaller, harder ball. Much of Spain's success in recent years is down to the team's reliable keeper Paños. Playing in her third World Cup, Paños has earned 50 appearances and can stand in as captain when called upon. She's great at making flying saves, organising her defence and guessing the right way when facing penalties.

COUNTRY: Spain
CLUB: Barcelona
BORN: 4 November, 1992
CAPS: 54

Paños started out as a futsal goalkeeper, a skilful game played with a smaller, harder ball.

MARY **EARPS**

Earps fought off competition from some talented young keepers to become England's no.1 under Sarina Wiegman. The commanding goalkeeper helped the *Lionesses* to qualify for the World Cup without letting in a single goal! She's brave when claiming crosses, fearless when diving at attackers' feet and super cool when facing penalties.

COUNTRY: England
CLUB: Manchester United
BORN: 7 March 1993
CAPS: 29

Ballet training as a child helped to build the keeper's grace and flexibility.

MERLE **FROHMS**

With her lightning-fast reflexes and skilled shot-stopping, Frohms is a safe pair of hands in Germany's goal. She is confident playing the ball out from the back to begin German attacks. The reserve keeper to Almuth Schult at France 2019, Frohms will be hoping to get her first taste of World Cup action on the pitch this time around.

COUNTRY: Germany
CLUB: Wolfsburg
BORN: 28 January 1995
CAPS: 36

ALYSSA **NAEHER**

A strong and powerful goalkeeper, Naeher will earn her third gold medal as a world champion if United States claim the FIFA Women's World Cup once more. She's not the type of player who screams at her defenders, but they know they can rely on her to pull off important saves when called into action.

COUNTRY: United States
CLUB: Chicago Red Stars
BORN: April 20 1988
CAPS: 86

Naeher and Germany keeper Schult kept the most clean sheets at France 2019 (four).

Frohms has won the UEFA Women's Champions League twice with Wolfsburg.

DEFENDERS

Good defenders love keeping out goals as much as forwards enjoy scoring them! These players know exactly how to snuff out danger, whether playing at full-back, wing-back or at the heart of the defence. Their height and power can add to the team's goal threat from attacking set pieces, too.

KADEISHA **BUCHANAN**

A solid stopper, centre-back Buchanan likes to break out from defence and carry the ball into midfield. The Canadian made her senior debut in 2013 while still at high school, and has since won an incredible number of international caps. This tournament will be Buchanan's third World Cup.

COUNTRY: Canada
CLUB: Chelsea
BORN: 5 November 1995
CAPS: 128
GOALS: 4

Buchanan won the Young Player Award at the FIFA Women's World Cup 2015™ in her home nation.

ELLIE **CARPENTER**

Still only 23, this young defender has already earned more than 50 caps for her country, after first starring for the *Matildas* aged just 15. Carpenter is a fast full-back, who loves to speed down the right wing and bolster the attack. Injured in May 2022, she is on course to recover in time to join the squad for her second World Cup.

COUNTRY: Australia
CLUB: Lyon
BORN: 28 April 2000
CAPS: 57
GOALS: 3

Carpenter has already played club football in Australia, United States and France's top leagues.

LEAH **WILLIAMSON**

England captain Williamson is a skilful defender who possesses perfect passing skills. She's always in the right position to swipe the ball away from attackers without having to make any crunching tackles. Her calming leadership will be important if the *Lionesses* are to push for a medal.

COUNTRY: England
CLUB: Arsenal
BORN: 29 March 1997
CAPS: 39
GOALS: 2

Williamson played every minute as she led England to glory at UEFA Women's EURO 2022.

RAFAELLE **SOUZA**

Captain Rafaelle is among Brazil's most experienced players and continues to lead by example from the centre of defence. Cool under pressure, her tackles are timed to perfection, while her strength and height give her the edge when she joins the attack. She's played club football in the United States, China and Brazil before joining English side Arsenal.

COUNTRY: Brazil
CLUB: Arsenal
BORN: 18 June 1991
CAPS: 13
GOALS: 1

Rafaelle first played at a World Cup in Canada 2015 but was ruled out of France 2019 by injury.

MIDFIELDERS

Midfielders link the team's defence and attack, and must have a whole range of skills, from defending and tackling to passing and shooting. Defensive midfielders break up the opposition's attacks and protect the defence. Attacking midfielders, on the other hand, try to create chances to score.

CATARINA **MACARIO**

Big things were predicted for midfielder Macario, and she has lived up to the hype so far! Her best position is as an attacking midfielder, where she can use her pace to beat defenders, conjure up chances or shoot at goal. A natural goalscorer, Macario is raring to play at her first World Cup.

COUNTRY: United States
CLUB: Lyon
BORN: October 4 1999
CAPS: 17
GOALS: 8

ALEXIA **PUTELLAS**

A brilliant attacking midfielder with unbeatable stats for goals and assists, Putellas runs the show at the heart of the Spanish midfield. The squad's sensational skipper became the first player to reach a century of caps for *La Roja* and has been key to Spain's success in recent years. Look out for her silky skills!

COUNTRY: Spain
CLUB: Barcelona
BORN: 4 February 1994
CAPS: 100
GOALS: 27

Brazilian-born Macario moved to San Diego, USA, at the age of 12 to pursue her football dream.

Putellas had to battle back from injury to be fit for her third World Cup.

LENA OBERDORF

One of the world's most exciting young players, Oberdorf pulls the strings in Germany's midfield. This defensive midfielder quickly shuts down attacks with her fearless tackles and always knows the right pass to play. This is her second World Cup, after being selected for France 2019, aged just 17.

COUNTRY: Germany
CLUB: Wolfsburg
BORN: 19 December 2001
CAPS: 35
GOALS: 3

KEIRA WALSH

As England's playmaker, Walsh is always looking to make killer passes that unlock defences and put her team-mates through on goal. With top technique and fantastic vision, she's one of the best central midfielders in the game. Playing in her second World Cup, Walsh hopes to make a big impact in the tournament.

COUNTRY: England
CLUB: Barcelona
BORN: 8 April 1997
CAPS: 54
GOALS: 0

Oberdorf received her first senior Germany call-up when she was still at school!

Walsh became the most expensive women's player when she moved to Barcelona in September 2022.

FORWARDS

Whether a team lines up with a single striker or up to three fearsome forwards, these attack-minded players must convert chances to make the collective hard work count. Meet four forwards hoping their goals will fire their sides to World Cup glory.

DEBINHA

A fabulous forward with fantastic footwork, Debinha has stepped out of the shadows of some of Brazil's all-time greats to become one of the team's top players. With over 120 caps, her experience and ability to play in a number of attacking roles will be key to Brazil's success in Australia and Aotearoa New Zealand.

COUNTRY: Brazil
CLUB: Kansas City Current
BORN: 20 October 1991
CAPS: 129
GOALS: 57

Debinha dazzles with her driving runs down the wing.

ALEX MORGAN

Known for her predator's instincts in the box, the two-time World Cup winner has been an incredible goalscorer for USA over the years – her record now stands at more than 120 international strikes. Morgan's hard work matches her natural ability in front of goal – qualities that saw the striker earn a spot at her fourth World Cup.

COUNTRY: United States
CLUB: San Diego Wave
BORN: 2 July 1989
CAPS: 204
GOALS: 121

Morgan is keen to reach double figures for goals scored at the FIFA Women's World Cup.

SAM **KERR**

Australia's ace striker Kerr will be gunning for the Golden Boot, as her home nation hosts the world. The *Matildas*' captain is already their all-time leading scorer, and can boast speed, athleticism and cool finishing among her top skills. This will be Kerr's fourth World Cup tournament, and she's yet to turn 30!

COUNTRY: Australia
CLUB: Chelsea
BORN: 10 September 1993
CAPS: 116
GOALS: 61

BUNNY **SHAW**

Jamaica's captain and all-time top scorer, Khadija 'Bunny' Shaw is an unstoppable striker when on form. She can finish with both feet and win headers in the air. Most incredibly, she reached 50 goals in just 36 appearances for the *Reggae Girlz*! Now she's set to take on the world's best defenders in her second World Cup.

COUNTRY: Jamaica
CLUB: Manchester City
BORN: 31 January 1997
CAPS: 38
GOALS: 56

No player, male or female, has scored more goals for Jamaica than Shaw.

Kerr has one of the best goal celebrations in the game – an acrobatic backflip!

PLAY TO WIN!

Test your skills as a super-duper fan of women's football with our quick quiz and picture puzzles.

© FIFA TM

HIGH SCORE

Ready to test your knowledge of the FIFA Women's World Cup? Tackle the questions yourself, then ask a friend to try to beat your score!

❶ Which of these teams have been previous champions?
- [ ] France
- [ ] Spain
- [ ] Germany
- [ ] England

❷ Where will the 2023 FIFA Women's World Cup final be played this summer?
- [ ] Melbourne
- [ ] Sydney
- [ ] Auckland

❸ How many teams had to qualify for the 2023 FIFA Women's World Cup in Australia and Aotearoa New Zealand?
- [ ] 28
- [ ] 30
- [ ] 32

❹ Which team is nicknamed the *Football Ferns*?
- [ ] Australia
- [ ] Italy
- [ ] Brazil
- [ ] New Zealand

❺ Which trophy is awarded to the best player in the competition?
- [ ] adidas Golden Boot
- [ ] adidas Golden Ball
- [ ] adidas Golden Glove

❻ Which of these star players is NOT a defender?
- [ ] Lena Oberdorf
- [ ] Ellie Carpenter
- [ ] Rafaelle Souza
- [ ] Leah Williamson

❼ Before the 2023 tournament, how many times had the USA won the FIFA Women's World Cup?
- [ ] 2
- [ ] 3
- [ ] 4

❽ Which player is NOT the leading scorer for her nation?
- [ ] Marta
- [ ] Beth Mead
- [ ] Sam Kerr
- [ ] Jennifer Hermoso

PARTY PIECE

Which super striker below is celebrating her goal in style? Rearrange the picture to find out.

CORRECT ORDER

A

B

C

D

E

...and the player is:

COUNTRY COLOURS

Colour in each jersey in the primary home colour of the country labelled underneath.

Spain

Nigeria

France

Australia

Netherlands

The answers are at the back of the book.

✓

MEET THE TOP TEAMS:

AUSTRALIA

With their home advantage, Australia may never have a better chance of reaching the later knockout rounds this summer. Caitlin Foord's exciting wing play will be the key to unlocking defences, while expectations will be on captain Sam Kerr to grab plenty of goals up front. Beaten in the round of 16 at France 2019, the *Matildas* are looking to improve this time around.

COACH: Tony Gustavsson (Sweden)

CAPTAIN: Sam Kerr

MOST CAPS: Cheryl Salisbury/Clare Polkinghorne (151)

TOP SCORER: Sam Kerr (61)

WORLD CUP APPEARANCES: 8

BEST FINISH: Quarter-finals (2007, 2011, 2015)

PLAYER SPOTLIGHT

Forward Caitlin Foord was named Best Women's Young Player at the 2011 tournament when she was only 16.

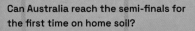

Can Australia reach the semi-finals for the first time on home soil?

MEET THE TOP TEAMS:

🇧🇷 BRAZIL

Brazil enter the tournament without some of their stars from past tournaments, so the next generation must be ready to step into their boots. The *Seleção* (The National Squad) have played in every World Cup, winning silver and bronze medals, but never the famous trophy itself. Pia Sundhage's side will need to be on top form to reach the final.

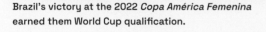

Brazil's victory at the 2022 *Copa América Femenina* earned them World Cup qualification.

COACH: Pia Sundhage (Sweden)

CAPTAIN: Marta

MOST CAPS: Formiga (206)

TOP SCORER: Marta (115)

WORLD CUP APPEARANCES: 9

BEST FINISH: Runners-up (2007)

PLAYER SPOTLIGHT

Goal-getter Geyse de Silva Ferreira, known as Geyse, featured for Brazil at France 2019.

MEET THE TOP TEAMS:

🍁 CANADA

With top players including defensive duo Ashley Lawrence and Kadeisha Buchanan, plus goal queen Christine Sinclair, Canada are among the strongest teams in the world. If Bev Preistman's stars make the most of their potential, *Les Rouges* have every chance of featuring in the semi-finals for the first time since 2003.

COACH: Bev Priestman (England)

CAPTAIN: Christine Sinclair

MOST CAPS: Christine Sinclair (319)

TOP SCORER: Christine Sinclair (190)

WORLD CUP APPEARANCES: 8

BEST FINISH: Fourth place (2003)

Canada have only missed one FIFA Women's World Cup – the first ever tournament held in 1991.

PLAYER SPOTLIGHT

Jessie Fleming is a classy midfielder who can handle high-pressure matches.

MEET THE TOP TEAMS:

✚ ENGLAND

Having beaten the best sides in Europe to become European champions, the *Lionesses* must now take on the world. Semi-finalists at France 2019, England's success at a major tournament and their winning mentality could see them reach the final in Sydney. For half the squad, though, it will be their first experience of playing at a World Cup.

England had a perfect record in qualification, taking maximum points without letting in a single goal.

PLAYER SPOTLIGHT
After her stunning goals at EURO 2022, will Alessia Russo lead the line at the World Cup in 2023?

COACH: Sarina Wiegman (Netherlands)

CAPTAIN: Leah Williamson

MOST CAPS: Fara Williams (172)

TOP SCORER: Ellen White (52)

WORLD CUP APPEARANCES: 6

BEST FINISH: Third place (2015)

FRANCE

A squad full of flair players, France must discover their best line-up and summon the mental courage that will take them far in the tournament. First, *Les Bleues* face tricky opponents Brazil and Jamaica in the Group Stage and will need forwards Baltimore and Sarr to step up and score the goals.

COACH: Corinne Diacre (France)

CAPTAIN: Charlotte Bilbault

MOST CAPS: Sandrine Soubeyrand (198)

TOP SCORER: Eugénie Le Sommer (86)

WORLD CUP APPEARANCES: 5

BEST FINISH: 4th (2011)

PLAYER SPOTLIGHT

Midfielder Grace Geyoro has developed into one of France's most important players.

France's best performance was at Germany 2011, where they reached the semi-finals.

GERMANY

With a squad that boasts big-game experience and exciting new talent, Germany will no doubt be hard to beat in Australia and Aotearoa New Zealand. Captain Alexandra Popp leads the line, while Lina Magull and Sara Däbritz play alongside the impressive young Lena Oberdorf in midfield. Anything less than a semi-final place would be a major disappointment for Germany fans.

COACH: Martina Voss-Tecklenburg (Germany)

CAPTAIN: Alexandra Popp

MOST CAPS: Birgit Prinz (214)

TOP SCORER: Birgit Prinz (128)

WORLD CUP APPEARANCES: 9

BEST FINISH: Champions (2003, 2007)

Germany have not reached a World Cup final since China 2007, where they claimed their second title.

PLAYER SPOTLIGHT

Germany captain Alexandra Popp is hoping to put her run of bad luck with injuries behind her.

● JAPAN

Japan stunned the world when they beat the United States to become the first Asian nation to win the FIFA Women's World Cup in 2011, and finished as runners-up in 2015. Saki Kumagai captains the team, one of just a handful of Japanese stars who play their football abroad. Expect to see a well-drilled side, who are willing to defend patiently until a chance to score comes up.

Japan were knocked out by the Netherlands in the round of 16 at France 2019.

COACH: Futoshi Ikeda (Japan)

CAPTAIN: Saki Kumagai

MOST CAPS: Homare Sawa (205)

TOP SCORER: Homare Sawa (83)

WORLD CUP APPEARANCES: 9

BEST FINISH: Champions (2011)

PLAYER SPOTLIGHT

Creative forward Mana Iwabuchi first played for her country at 16 and was a World Cup winner with Japan aged just 18.

NETHERLANDS

Netherlands pipped Iceland to top spot in their qualifying group with a 93rd minute winner to seal a place at only their third World Cup finals. A team packed with talent in every position, many of the finalists from France 2019 feature once again, alongside fresh new starlets including keeper Daphne van Domselaar and forward Esmee Brugts.

COACH: Andries Jonker (Netherlands)

CAPTAIN: Sherida Spitse

MOST CAPS: Sherida Spitse (206)

TOP SCORER: Vivianne Miedema (95)

WORLD CUP APPEARANCES: 3

BEST FINISH: Runners-up (2019)

Can the Netherlands make it to back-to-back World Cup finals in 2023?

PLAYER SPOTLIGHT

Dynamic midfielder Jill Roord has her sights set on playing in her third FIFA Women's World Cup.

NEW ZEALAND

Jointly hosting the tournament with Australia, New Zealand face a stern test if they are to progress to the knockout stages and will rely on the support of their home fans to spur them on. The *Football Ferns* have never made it beyond the group stage in five tournament appearances so far, but their squad boasts players from some of the world's top leagues.

Hannah Wilkinson (back row, second from left) is the current squad's leading goalscorer.

PLAYER SPOTLIGHT

American-born defender Ali Riley will captain the side in what could be her fourth and final tournament.

COACH: Jitka Klimková (Czech Republic)

CAPTAIN: Ali Riley

MOST CAPS: Ria Percival (160)

TOP SCORER: Amber Hearn (54)

WORLD CUP APPEARANCES: 6

BEST FINISH: Group stage (1991, 2007, 2011, 2015, 2019)

SPAIN

A nation that has rocketed up the world rankings since France 2019, Spain play an attractive attacking style of football. *La Roja* have only qualified for two World Cup tournaments previously, in 2015 and 2019, but have a squad of superstars aiming to make up for lost time in Australia and Aotearoa New Zealand. Their midfield ace, Alexia Putellas, was named the Best FIFA Women's Player in 2021.

COACH: Jorge Vilda (Spain)

CAPTAIN: Irene Paredes

MOST CAPS: Alexia Putellas (100)

TOP SCORER: Jennifer Hermoso (46)

WORLD CUP APPEARANCES: 3

BEST FINISH: Round of 16 (2019)

Spain have not yet reached the quarter-finals of a FIFA Women's World Cup.

PLAYER SPOTLIGHT

Attacking midfielder Aitana Bonmatí has been central to Spain's development, with an outstanding goals and assists record.

MEET THE TOP TEAMS:

🇸🇪 SWEDEN

Bronze medallists at France 2019, Sweden are aiming to reach a first final since 2003. Sweden rank as one of the best sides in the world, and head to Australia and Aotearoa New Zealand with high hopes. Players set to star for the *Blågult* include defenders Hanna Glas and Magdalena Eriksson, as well as their dangerous top scorer Kosovare Asllani.

Sweden feature near the very top of the official FIFA/Coca-Cola Women's World Rankings.

PLAYER SPOTLIGHT

Playing in her second FIFA Women's World Cup, striker Stina Blackstenius is known for scoring timely goals.

COACH: Peter Gerhardsson (Sweden)

CAPTAIN: Caroline Seger

MOST CAPS: Caroline Seger (229)

TOP SCORER: Lotta Schelin (88)

WORLD CUP APPEARANCES: 9

BEST FINISH: Runners-up (2003)

MEET THE TOP TEAMS:

 **USA**

When it comes to winning, no team has more experience than USA. The four-time champions' squad includes many players with gold medals from Canada 2015 and France 2019, including Megan Rapinoe and Alex Morgan. Some talented newcomers also feature for the *Stars and Stripes*, all hoping to reach their first final in Sydney.

COACH: Vlatko Andonovski (USA)

CAPTAIN: Becky Sauerbrunn

MOST CAPS: Kristine Lilly (354)

TOP SCORER: Abby Wambach (184)

WORLD CUP APPEARANCES: 9

BEST FINISH: Champions (1991, 1999, 2015, 2019)

PLAYER SPOTLIGHT

The creative young forward Trinity Rodman continues to impress after making her senior USA debut at the 2022 SheBelieves Cup.

Could United States become the first team to win a historic three titles in a row?

MY FIFA WOMEN'S WORLD CUP DREAM TEAM

Once the tournament is over, it's time to decide which players starred as the very best in the world! From dazzling defenders to amazing attackers, choose 11 players to make up your team of the tournament.

© FIFA TM

FORMATIONS EXPLAINED . . .

4-3-3

This pitch shows players lined up in a 4-3-3 formation, with four defenders, three centre midfielders and a trio of forwards. The system is perfect for teams that love to keep possession, have strong passers of the ball and tricky wingers. United States set up this way to win the trophy at France 2019.

4-2-3-1

Two defensive midfielders line up In front of four defenders, with three attacking midfielders and a lone striker furthest forward. England used this formation to become European champions, making the most of the team's creative attacking players, while staying strong in defence.

3-5-2

Three central defenders are supported by two energetic wing-backs, who drop back from midfield to help defend when the opposition attacks. At the top of the formation, two strikers work hard to press the ball and win possession.

4-4-2

The 4-4-2 formation is made up of four defenders, four midfielders and two strikers. Teams play in a more direct style, soaking up the pressure, before attacking on the break. The four midfielders sometimes set up in a diamond shape. Japan favour this formation.

© FIFA TM

Goalkeepers aren't counted in formations as their position is fixed.

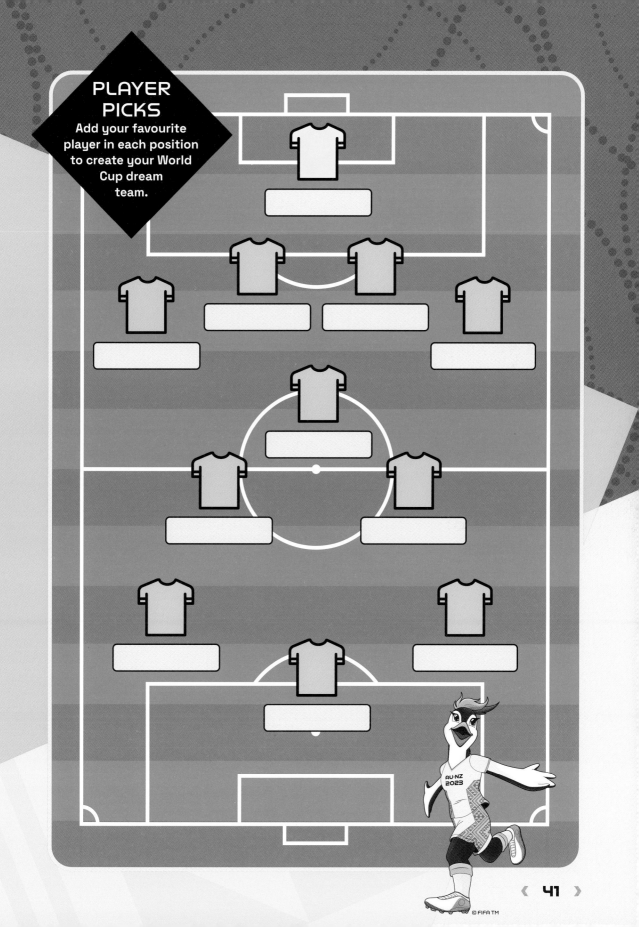

PLAYER PICKS

Add your favourite player in each position to create your World Cup dream team.

© FIFA TM

GROUP STAGE

Add the teams and scores for each match after the final whistle is blown, then complete the final group tables. The top two teams from each group head straight to the round of 16.

Group A

20 Jul	08:00	New Zealand ◯ v ◯ Norway	Auckland
21 Jul	06:00	Philippines ◯ v ◯ Switzerland	Dunedin
25 Jul	06:30	New Zealand ◯ v ◯ Philippines	Wellington
25 Jul	09:00	Switzerland ◯ v ◯ Norway	Hamilton
30 Jul	08:00	Switzerland ◯ v ◯ New Zealand	Dunedin
30 Jul	08:00	Norway ◯ v ◯ Philippines	Auckland

Group A table

	Team	P	W	D	L	G	D	Pts
1								
2								
3								
4								

Group B

20 Jul	11:00	Australia ◯ v ◯ Rep. Ireland	Sydney
21 Jul	03:30	Nigeria ◯ v ◯ Canada	Melbourne
26 Jul	13:00	Canada ◯ v ◯ Rep. Ireland	Perth
27 Jul	11:00	Australia ◯ v ◯ Nigeria	Brisbane
31 Jul	11:00	Canada ◯ v ◯ Australia	Melbourne
31 Jul	11:00	Rep. Ireland ◯ v ◯ Nigeria	Brisbane

Group B table

	Team	P	W	D	L	G	D	Pts
1								
2								
3								
4								

Group C

21 Jul	08:30	Spain ◯ v ◯ Costa Rica	Wellington
22 Jul	08:00	Zambia ◯ v ◯ Japan	Hamilton
26 Jul	06:00	Japan ◯ v ◯ Costa Rica	Dunedin
26 Jul	08:30	Spain ◯ v ◯ Zambia	Auckland
31 Jul	08:00	Japan ◯ v ◯ Spain	Wellington
31 Jul	08:00	Costa Rica ◯ v ◯ Zambia	Hamilton

Group C table

	Team	P	W	D	L	G	D	Pts
1								
2								
3								
4								

Group D

22 Jul	10:30	England ◯ v ◯	Brisbane
22 Jul	13:00	Denmark ◯ v ◯ China PR	Perth
28 Jul	09:30	England ◯ v ◯ Denmark	Sydney
28 Jul	12:00	China PR ◯ v ◯	Adelaide
1 Aug	12:00	China PR ◯ v ◯ England	Adelaide
1 Aug	12:00	◯ v ◯ Denmark	Perth

Group D table

	Team	P	W	D	L	G	D	Pts
1								
2								
3								
4								

Please note: all kick-off times are BST.

Group E

22 Jul	02:00	United States	◯ v ◯	Vietnam	Auckland
23 Jul	08:30	Netherlands	◯ v ◯		Dunedin
27 Jul	02:00	United States	◯ v ◯	Netherlands	Wellington
27 Jul	08:30		◯ v ◯	Vietnam	Hamilton
1 Aug	08:00		◯ v ◯	United States	Auckland
1 Aug	08:00	Vietnam	◯ v ◯	Netherlands	Dunedin

Group E table

Team	P	W	D	L	G	D	Pts
1							
2							
3							
4							

Group F

23 Jul	11:00	France	◯ v ◯	Jamaica	Sydney
24 Jul	12:00	Brazil	◯ v ◯		Adelaide
29 Jul	11:00	France	◯ v ◯	Brazil	Brisbane
29 Jul	13:30		◯ v ◯	Jamaica	Perth
2 Aug	11:00		◯ v ◯	France	Sydney
2 Aug	11:00	Jamaica	◯ v ◯	Brazil	Melbourne

Group F table

Team	P	W	D	L	G	D	Pts
1							
2							
3							
4							

Group G

23 Jul	06:00	Sweden	◯ v ◯	South Africa	Wellington
24 Jul	07:00	Italy	◯ v ◯	Argentina	Auckland
28 Jul	01:00	Argentina	◯ v ◯	South Africa	Dunedin
29 Jul	08:30	Sweden	◯ v ◯	Italy	Wellington
2 Aug	08:00	Argentina	◯ v ◯	Sweden	Hamilton
2 Aug	08:00	South Africa	◯ v ◯	Italy	Wellington

Group G table

Team	P	W	D	L	G	D	Pts
1							
2							
3							
4							

Group H

24 Jul	09:30	Germany	◯ v ◯	Morocco	Melbourne
25 Jul	03:00	Colombia	◯ v ◯	Korea Rep.	Sydney
30 Jul	05:30	Korea Rep.	◯ v ◯	Morocco	Adelaide
30 Jul	10:30	Germany	◯ v ◯	Colombia	Sydney
3 Aug	11:00	Korea Rep.	◯ v ◯	Germany	Brisbane
3 Aug	11:00	Morocco	◯ v ◯	Colombia	Perth

Group H table

Team	P	W	D	L	G	D	Pts
1							
2							
3							
4							

Please note: all kick-off times are BST.

ROUND OF 16

Only half the teams remain following the group stage. The round of 16 is the start of the knockout stage.

R16 Match 1   Winner Group A   Runner-up Group C

5 Aug   06:00   ⚪ v ⚪   Auckland

Goalscorers

R16 Match 2   Winner Group C   Runner-up Group A

5 Aug   09:00   ⚪ v ⚪   Wellington

Goalscorers

R16 Match 3   Winner Group E   Runner-up Group G

6 Aug   03:00   ⚪ v ⚪   Sydney

Goalscorers

R16 Match 4   Winner Group G   Runner-up Group E

6 Aug   10:00   ⚪ v ⚪   Melbourne

Goalscorers

R16 Match 5   Winner Group B   Runner-up Group D

7 Aug   11:30   ⚪ v ⚪   Sydney

Goalscorers

R16 Match 6   Winner Group D   Runner-up Group B

7 Aug   08:30   ⚪ v ⚪   Brisbane

Goalscorers

R16 Match 7   Winner Group F   Runner-up Group H

8 Aug   12:00   ⚪ v ⚪   Adelaide

Goalscorers

R16 Match 8   Winner Group H   Runner-up Group F

8 Aug   09:00   ⚪ v ⚪   Melbourne

Goalscorers

Please note: all kick-off times are BST.

QUARTER-FINALS

Eight teams feature in the quarter-finals, with the winner from each tie forming the final four nations battling it out to win the famous trophy.

Quarter-final A Winner R16 Match 1 Winner R16 Match 3

11 Aug 02:00 v Wellington

Goalscorers

Quarter-final B Winner R16 Match 2 Winner R16 Match 4

11 Aug 08:30 v Auckland

Goalscorers

Quarter-final C Winner R16 Match 5 Winner R16 Match 7

12 Aug 08:00 v Brisbane

Goalscorers

Quarter-final D Winner R16 Match 6 Winner R16 Match 8

12 Aug 11:30 v Sydney

Goalscorers

Netherlands' Stefanie van der Gragt celebrates her goal against Italy in the 2019 quarter-final.

SEMI-FINALS

Four teams left! The winners of each semi-final match reach the final, while the two runners-up still have a chance to earn bronze medals.

Semi-final I	Winner quarter-final A		Winner quarter-final B	
15 Aug 09:00		v		Auckland
		Goalscorers		

Semi-final II	Winner quarter-final C		Winner quarter-final D	
16 Aug 11:00		v		Sydney
		Goalscorers		

Third place Play-off	Runner-up semi-final I		Runner-up semi-final II	
19 Aug 09:00		v		Brisbane
		Goalscorers		

USA's Alex Morgan celebrates scoring her second goal against England during the 2019 semi-final match.